ISBN 978-1-331-30637-5
PIBN 10171996

1 MONTH OF
FREE
READING

at

www.ForgottenBooks.com

By purchasing this book you are eligible for one month membership to ForgottenBooks.com, giving you unlimited access to our entire collection of over 700,000 titles via our web site and mobile apps.

To claim your free month visit:

www.forgottenbooks.com/free171996

Similar Books Are Available from
www.forgottenbooks.com

OLD NEW ENGLAND HOUSES

BY

ALBERT G. ROBINSON

AUTHOR OF "OLD NEW ENGLAND DOORWAYS"

WITH MANY ILLUSTRATIONS
FROM THE AUTHOR'S UNIQUE COLLECTION OF PHOTOGRAPHS

NEW YORK
CHARLES SCRIBNER'S SONS
1920

A491167

NA

7210

PLATES

[v]

PLATES

PLATES

PLATES

OLD NEW ENGLAND
HOUSES

OLD NEW ENGLAND HOUSES

THE homes of the earliest settlers in New England were log huts small in size and rude in construction—

"Of such materials as around,
The workman's hand had readiest found;
Lopp'd of their boughs, their hoar trunks bared,
And with the hatchet rudely squared."
SCOTT, *Lady of the Lake.*

The chinks between the logs, due to the uneven surfacing, were filled with clay or mud. The roofs were thatch. The floor was the little section of the earth's surface enclosed within the walls or, at best, the flat side of split logs, rudely dressed, known as puncheons. Most of the furniture was only what the occupant could fashion with axe and saw. The fireplace, as a writer has cleverly described it, "sent half the smoke into the apartment and half the heat up the chimney." For a short time one room, in many cases, served for all purposes. These simple structures afforded the necessary shelter, but the

[3]

New England colonists were not of a class content to live in so rude a manner. Lumber, both hand sawed and mill-sawed, was produced soon after their arrival. The earliest mill of which I find record was erected in the vicinity of Portsmouth in 1631 by a man named Gibbons. But the output of the little mills of the early days was limited in quantity, and a number of generations passed before the log hut disappeared. As the pioneers pushed their way, year after year, into the interior, northward and westward, they built in western Massachusetts, in Maine, New Hampshire, and Vermont, log cabins such as were built in an earlier day in the coast settlements and along the valleys of the larger rivers. For them, as for the first settlers, shelter was a requirement second only to food, and the readiest means of meeting the necessity was the cutting, hewing, and piling of logs from the surrounding forest. Even after the operation of sawmills, much of the heavier framing timber was hewn from logs. This is often revealed when the old houses are torn down or altered.

Several houses whose erection is credibly reported as prior to 1640 are still standing. Some are one story and some are two stories in height. The destruction a few years ago of the old house in St. Augustine doubtless leaves some ancient New England structure as "the oldest house in the United States." It is perhaps impossible to determine which one of the several claimants is rightfully .entitled to the distinction. The claim has been made for the Fairbanks house in Dedham, Mass a part of which was built in 1636. The genealogist of the Caldwell family claims 1633 as the date of the Caldwell homestead which stands on High Street in Ipswich. Some have claimed 1633 for the old Whipple house in the same town. Again, the oldest house may be still standing with no record to prove its antiquity. Errors in the matter of dates are frequent enough. A date quite impossible, as proven by the architectural type or the character of the workmanship, is often given, in all honesty, by the occupant of a house. In some instances the date given is that of the erection of a more modest structure that has given place to the present building or that serves as an ell or extension to the newer part. It is not unusual to find a really old house with an older structure attached, the date of all being given as that of the oldest part.

Year by year the number of these old-time homes lessens. They burn down, fall down, or are torn down. Some are "improved" by the addition of a veranda, a bay window, a modern door, or by the substitution of large window-panes for the old diamond panes or the much more common but less ancient six-by-eight panes. There are still many of the real "old-timers" to be found, but more and more, from year to year, it becomes necessary to hunt for them. Some, though only a fraction of them, are more or less well known, and have been used repeatedly as illustrations. But the tendency of illustrators has been to show a limited number of selected "mansion houses" rather than the homes in which a far greater number of people lived their quiet and inconspicuous lives. In the selected group are the stately homes in Salem and in Portsmouth, the Lee house in Marblehead, the Royall house in Medford, the Dummer house in Byfield, the "Lindens" in Danvers, the Longfellow and Lowell houses in Cambridge, and a few others of particularly interesting history or of special architectural merit. In another group of selected structures appear the familiar Fairbanks house in Dedham, the Frary house in Deerfield, the Whipple house in

Ipswich, the Tallmadge house in Litchfield, the Wayside Inn, and a few others. All of these, in both groups, are excellent for the purposes for which they are used, but they present, after all, only a few out of the many old houses that still remain widely scattered through the southern half of New England.

The hunt for these old structures resolves itself into a somewhat general and elastic system, a location of areas in which the hunt is likely to prove fruitful or otherwise. Thus, in some of the oldest settlements little remains in the way of the oldest architecture. This is particularly true of the larger cities, of Boston, Providence, Newport, Hartford, New Haven, and Springfield. On the sites of the homes of the people of the seventeenth century, and of a large part of the eighteenth, stand the brick and the stone piles of the nineteenth and the twentieth centuries. The old has given place to the new. In the vicinity of those cities there is a fair hunting-field although "modern improvement" has in many instances converted charming old houses into architectural jumbles seldom pleasing and often little short of offensive. Very much the same is true of a number of smaller cities such as

Northampton, Holyoke, New London, and Haverhill. A somewhat larger restriction appears in the distinction between the northern and southern portions of the region. Massachusetts, Connecticut, and Rhode Island had a long start, more than a hundred years, over Vermont and all except a small area of New Hampshire and of Maine. It was not until after the French and Indian War, finally terminated by the Treaty of Paris in 1763, that more than a mere corner of those States was safe for settlers.

On the other hand, certain places are found to be of notable fruitfulness. Connecticut has several such centres, including Guilford, Farmington, Windsor, Litchfield, and Wethersfield. Rhode Island has Warren, Bristol, Wickford, and others. Massachusetts has Concord and Lexington, Ipswich, Deerfield and Hadley, and a few more. With the exception of Farmington and Litchfield, in both of which the "mansion house," or "near mansion house," type is prominent, the old-time houses in these places were the homes of those of comparatively limited but still comfortable income. It is the hunt for houses of that class that really affords the greatest pleasure and interest. The hunter never knows where he may come upon a building that will make a notable addition to his collection. As a matter of fact, however, only a part of them are worth collecting. Age may not be the only determining factor in the hunter's interest. Without a second glance, I have passed many houses that were undoubtedly well along toward the end of their second century. What is the hunter's test for his collection? Naturally, that varies with the individual taste or special purpose of the hunter. Not long ago I made an excursion through a fruitful region with an architect. Had time permitted, he would have spent hours, with rule and note-book, measuring and recording details of houses at which I did not care to point a camera. Mere age might be the standard for some; grace of line and charm of proportion for others; while for others, perhaps including myself, selection would be determined mainly by what may be called the "picture quality." To those of the latter class appeal might be made by a house of no particular architectural merit, but of respectable age, if it stood under the shade of a sweeping elm or was flanked by noble maples. To others the history of a house may be the feature of interest. Did Washington or Lafayette sleep in it? Was it the birthplace or the sometime home of a distinguished soldier in the Revolutionary War? Did any notable person ever live in it or stay in it? Just that is the charm of hunting for old houses. The search presents so many sides, so many different lines of interest. Not the least of these is in being outdoors in a land of hills and valleys and running streams, of singing birds and wayside flowers.

How old must a house be to come properly into the class of "old houses"? As a rule, not less than a hundred years. Of course, nothing in this country except the country itself is really old. The term is distinctly relative. The houses that we call "old" are old only in comparison with those of more recent construction. Asking for old houses in some neighborhood then being hunted over, my attention has often been called to houses built about the middle of the nineteenth century, houses with the mansard roof and square tower that prevailed in what has been called the "Iron Dog Period of American Architecture." Happily, most of the iron dogs, the Dianas, the Apollo Belvederes, and the other cast-iron monstrosities, at one time supposed to be highly effective lawn decorations, have gone to the scrap-heap. No hard and fast rule of age limit can be .applied properly, but a century may be adopted as a general standard for another reason than that of time. During the latter part of the first quarter of the nineteenth century there came a marked change in public taste in the matter of architectural style. As that which may be called the Colonial period of American architecture was followed by the several stages of Georgian, so were they, about 1820, followed by an enthusiasm for the Classic. While this is most clearly shown in a number of familiar public buildings, its influence extended to private residences and is easily recognized. The transition from the later Georgian to the Classic produced some of the best designs in the entire range of American architecture, represented, in part, by the work of such men as Bulfinch and McIntire. Following them, though with more leaning to the Classic and less to the Georgian, came Latrobe, Hoban, Strickland, and others, whose work stands to-day distinguished for its combination of grace and dignity.

But all this matter of styles and periods has little to do with the homes in which the great majority of the early New Englanders spent their lives.

The extent of exterior decoration, for most of them, went no further than a more or less elaborate front doorway, and many had not even that. Through out New England may be found to-day hundreds of houses, plain, one or two story rectangular boxes with sloping covers. They vary in size, in the proportions of height to width in both front and side elevations, and in the angle of the roof. Some have passed their second century—and show it. Many are well preserved and, as far as their physical appearance is concerned, give no sign of their antiquity except to the trained eye, and even that is sometimes deceived. They are rejuvenated, in outward show, by shingles, clapboards, paint, new doors, and new window-sashes. Not infrequently, they look quite as modern as their fifty-year-old neighbors. Sometimes, too, even the fairly expert eye is misled by a modern house built in imitation of an old one. Still more deceptive are those that have been skilfully restored during recent years. For the increasing number of these expert restorations, let us be properly thankful. They include not only recovery from dilapidation, and even from wreck, but, as well, the displacement of the various abominations attached, notably within the last hundred years, with a lamentably mistaken notion of "improving the property."

Brick and stone, for house-building, came into use in a limited way at an early date. There is a fairly supported account of a brick house built in Boston in 1638, and there seems to be no reason to doubt that bricks were made in Salem as early as 1629, about a year after the arrival of Endicott. The two-story stone house, known as the Whitfield house, in Guilford, Conn., dates from 1639. This structure has been bought by the State and "restored." Somewhat unfortunately, perhaps, its restoration and the concealment of its walls and lines behind a mass of vines rob it of the external evidences of its age.

Many of the old two-story houses show the second-story "overhang" that Doctor Holmes said was a device that enabled the occupants of the house to shoot directly down at Indians who might be "knocking at the front door with their tomahawks." That is a picturesque but quite inaccurate explanation of that particular feature of early New England architecture. It may, at times, have served for that purpose, but it was, in fact, merely a transplanted system of house carpentry common enough in the

England from which came the builders, who naturally followed in the new land the methods with which they were familiar in the old land. That the custom was of mechanical and not of military origin has been amply proven by architects and antiquarians. This "overhang" varies in width but in the majority of cases is only a few inches. Sometimes it appears only on the front of the house, the projection at the rear being hidden by the roof line of the "lean-to." Somewhat less frequently it appears at the ends of the house as well as on the front. Not infrequently, on two-story houses, a second "overhang" appears at the eaves line on the end of the house. Here and there a house shows a wide overhang ornamented with pendants, as in the case of the Whitman house in Farmington, Conn., and the Brown house in Hamilton, Mass. The old bakery in Salem, the Porter house in Hadley, and a number of others have brackets under the overhang.

These old houses may be divided, broadly, into four groups, the difference being marked by the roof. One group includes the buildings, whether of one or two stories, with sloping roof of equal length in front and back, mere rectangular boxes

of varying size and proportions, with a doubly sloping cover. These are commonly known as "gable"
or "pitch" roof houses. Not a few of this type
show an attached ell, but in most cases, if not in all,
this is a later addition. A second group shows the
"lean-to" with the extension of the roof line in the
rear. While much more common to houses of two
stories in front, the long back roof appears occasionally on houses of a single story. A third group
includes the "gambrels." In his poem, "Parson
Turell's Legacy," Doctor Holmes gives the origin of
the term:

> " 'Gambrel?—Gambrel?' Let me beg
> You'll look at a horse's hinder leg,—
> First great angle above the hoof,—
> That's the gambrel; hence gambrel-roof."

I am not prepared to say whether this is reliable
information or a product of the genial autocrat's
fertile imagination. But old houses with gambrel
roof are abundant in New England. The form is
used in quaint cottages and in stately mansions
like the "Dorothy Q" house in Quincy and a number of others. The design appears to have been
borrowed from the Dutch, but it was used in New
England as early as the last quarter of the seven-

teenth century. While the use of the dormer-win-
dow, common enough in the South, was unusual
in the North, it is of frequent occurrence on houses
with the gambrel roof, both one and two storied.
But there is a material and not fully explained differ
ence between the New England gambrel and its
prototype. The latter is quite the more graceful.
Its upper slope is much shorter and its lower slope
less steep than is the New England roof. While
grace is lost, the New Englander gained in area of
headroom in what was, in effect, a second story.
The fourth group consists of the pyramidal type or
"hip" roof, usually square boxes with the roof slop
ing from the four sides to a common centre. This
also shows variations in roof angle as related to the
wall of the house. Also, while in many cases the
four slopes met at a central peak, or stopped at the
walls of a large central chimney, in many other
cases they terminated at the edge of a flat platform
around which, frequently if not usually, a low rail-
ing or fencing was built.

In all of these general groups there are variations
and modifications. There is occasionally found, in
the first group, a variation that is sometimes called
the "sliced gable" in which the sharp angle of the

gable is cut away diagonally and a short roof slope takes its place. This type belongs properly in the hip-roof class. I recall no such exception in the "lean-to" group, but in the other three there are variations in which the upper part of the roof would seem to have been cut away and its place taken by the flat platform, usually railed. This is generally known as the "captain's walk." It is most common in the coast cities, and its origin is said to be found in the use of the platform as a lookout over the harbor by shipmasters or ship-owners occupying the house. Occasionally one will see a house, one or two storied, of the conventional sloping-roof type, with one or more dormer-windows. It is probable, however, that in most cases these were of later addition.

One of the variations in the hip-roof type appears in what is sometimes called the "monitor," a windowed superstructure of much too great an area to be regarded as a cupola. A variation of the gable roof is occasionally encountered in southeastern Massachusetts. It is known as the "rain bow." The roof, from ridge-pole to eaves, instead of following a straight line, is slightly convex, thus making a few additional inches of headroom inside.

An interesting variation of type, unusual rather than rare, is the so-called "jut-by," in which the rear half of the house, sometimes of gable type and sometimes of the gambrel, extends several feet beyond the front half.

In most of the books dealing with early American architecture there appears an effort to classify the structures by periods. To most of us any house a hundred or more years old is "Colonial," and any house of later date, if it has an ornamental doorway, or columns or pilasters from ground to eaves, is of "Colonial" design. Some specialists employ a specific political grouping, thus: the Colonial, from the beginning until 1692; the Provincial, from 1692 until the Revolution; and the Federal, from that time until the Classic period, about 1820. Others divide by groups marked by distinct features of technical details. Still others use, broadly: the Colonial from the beginning until the Revolution; then the Georgian until the Classic. For all the purposes of that vast majority of the inexpert, it seems to me desirable only that we do not confuse the Colonial type with the Georgian, and there is no date at which we may fix, even approximately, a dividing line. The strictly Colonial type, represented by all except a very small number of the houses of the seventeenth century, persisted throughout the eighteenth and well into the nineteenth. It was the oblong building, of one or two stories, with gable roof, with or without the lean-to. It was of the utmost simplicity. Very few of the seventeenth-century houses had even an ornamental doorway. The porch, portico, veranda, and bay window were all devices of a much later period. Few, if any, were even painted.

The so-called Georgian period had its beginning, broadly, about the end of the first quarter of the eighteenth century. Although the French, from Canada, with their Indian allies raided York, Maine, in 1691, Haverhill in 1697 and again in 1708, and Deerfield in 1704, while in 1675 and 1676 the Wampanoags and the Narragansetts swept through Massachusetts, leaving thirteen towns in ashes, and bringing fire and slaughter to forty other towns, it was felt that there was no longer serious danger of further attack, particularly in the larger coast towns. By that time, also, there were a considerable number of men who were, for their time, wealthy. Such, naturally, desired something more commodious and more ornate in the matter of residences. To that the simple Colonial type did not readily lend itself. My investigations lead me to a belief that elaboration in house architecture began with gambrel-roofed houses of much larger size than those formerly erected, and that this was followed by and largely gave place to the imposing and dignified "three-deckers" of Salem, Portsmouth, Portland, and Providence, where the best types of Georgian architecture in New England are to be found. A few good examples can be seen elsewhere, but there is nothing better than those in the cities mentioned.

In referring to houses of the strictly Colonial type, I have once or twice used the term "rectangular boxes with variously sloping covers." They were no more than that. Wherein, then, lies their charm ? for charm they undoubtedly have in many cases. It is to be sought in two directions, in accuracy of proportions and in the setting of the house. The proportions are determined by an almost exact relation of height to width and of relation of door and window openings to each other and to the house as a whole. A proper adjustment of height to width was possible because the occupants were content with low ceilings. High ceilings came somewhat later in the cities and still later in the country, but they came in larger houses in which the relation of height to width could be and was maintained. No finer proportions in house construction can be found than those of many an old "three-decker" in Salem, Providence, and elsewhere, or in stately gambrel-roofed houses that may be seen scattered through the country. The old-time cottages were low, measuring from ground to eaves, but they suggest coseyness and comfort rather than "squattiness." Put one of those little houses under an overshadowing elm, run a vine about its entrance plant a few shrubs and flowers in its front yard, and it nestles there challenging attention and ad miration. The elms and the maples, as external house decorations, supplemented by roses and lilacs, are distinct features in the New England landscape.

In a class quite distinct from that referred to in the foregoing comment stand the more imposing houses the best types of which are to be found in or not far from the coast cities. Among those who came to the new land were some who, for the period, might be regarded as rich. They and others made money after they came. They were, most of them, ship-builders, ship-owners, and merchants engaged in oversea commerce. In the last quarter of the seventeenth century a few of these wealthy citizens built houses on what was then, in this country, a colossal scale. All, I believe, are now gone, but they were represented by such houses as that built in Boston in 1679 by Peter Sergeant, merchant. The building was afterward known as the Province House, having been bought in 1716 by the Province of Massachusetts Bay as an official residence for the royal governors.* Years afterward it became a tavern and later on a theatre. Others of this class were the Cotton Mather house on Hanover Street and the Foster-Hutchinson house on Garden Court. All of these were in Boston.

At the end of the first hundred years of settlement and activity there were in New England a considerable number of men possessed of substantial fortunes. Others were rapidly acquiring fortunes. Some of them did as do men of wealth to-day—they built large and more or less elaborately ornate houses. Andrew Faneuil built one in Boston in 1709, and in the same place William Clark built about the year 1713 and Thomas Hancock built in 1737. All of these are gone. Survivals of the period, however, may be found in the Dummer house (1715)

* See Hawthorne's *Legends of the Province House.*

in Byfield, the Warner house (1723) in Portsmouth, and the Royall house (1732) in Medford. Most of the houses of this class were three-storied, flat-topped structures if in the city, while those in the country were largely of the two-storied and gambrel-roofed type. But the gable roof, as shown by the Dummer house, was also represented. More and more of the "mansion houses" came in the last half of the eighteenth century, and many remain for our admiration to-day.

Not all of these "mansion" or "semi-mansion" houses were built of brick, nor were all located in the coast cities. There were three-story wooden houses and, of the same material, large two-story houses surmounted by gambrel roofs with dormer-windows. In the latter group are several houses in Litchfield, the Ropes house in Salem, the Dickinson house in Hadley, and numerous others variously located. As already stated, the best in American house architecture remains from the successive stages of the so-called Georgian period. But it is represented only in part by the "mansion" type and only in part by the buildings along the coast. The inland cities and towns have their many homes of a comfortable, well-to-do group of farmers and

[23]

traders. I know of no larger or better field for buildings of this class than the Naugatuck valley, in Connecticut, and its immediate neighborhood. There were still the many who built their little one-story houses with gable roof or gambrel and others who could afford a larger house, plain and substantial, usually of timber construction, although stone or brick structures are not infrequent.

Broadly, then, the era of development in American architecture had its beginning in the early years of the eighteenth century. Prior to that the type was simple and the building plain. The development was slow in its beginning, here and there a house that exceeded its neighbors in size and in the building of which some attention was given to ornamentation by doorway and window trim. The change from the simple type of the seventeenth century had its origin at the top. A wealthy man built a mansion. His well-to-do neighbor followed and built according to his means. A pace was set for all classes. The much greater wealth and the greater number of the wealthy made possible in the last half and more particularly in the last quarter of the eighteenth century and the early years of the nineteenth the erection of houses that in grace

OLD NEW ENGLAND HOUSES

and grandeur somewhat overshadowed the efforts of the earlier generations. As the Dummer house and the Warner house outclassed their neighbors in their day, so the Dodge-Shreve (1817) and the Andrew-Safford (1818) houses in Salem, the Ives (1799) and the Gammell (1786) houses in Provi dence, the Lee house in Marblehead, and various others outclassed the Dummer and the Warner buildings. Architecturally, there was an upward movement all through the eighteenth century. Yet, while we may look with all respect and admiration upon the stately mansions of Salem, Providence, and other cities, it is, after all, the old-time house or cottage, with its bit of shrubbery and garden and its flanking elms and maples, that most pleases our eyes and most warms our hearts.

Every old house has its history. In most cases it is not a history of public men or public events. It is only a record of generation after generation of simple human lives with their joys and sorrows, their little romances and little tragedies. Probably, few of us ever see the inside of these old houses. Usually, in a quiet and unostentatious fashion, the occupants are very proud of their possessions. Often the house has been kept in the family generation after generation, each adding to the collection of furniture, crockery, silverware and pewter, portraits and house equipment. My evident interest in the outside of some old house has repeatedlv led to an invitation to inspect its interior and many a pleasant hour has been so spent. Not infrequently the elaborate beauty of an interior trim, of mantels and door-casing, does not correspond with the simplicity of the exterior. Writing upon that point, an observer has declared that this lack of correspondence between the external and the internal "reflects the outward reserve and restraint of New England character, a reserve, however, that often melts into cordial geniality under the favoring auspices of a close acquaintance." I recall a delightful hour with a dear old soul, of perhaps seventy-five years of age, who, somewhat stiffly at first, asked me to come in. In a few minutes she had warmed herself and roused me to a fair pitch of enthusiasm over her old house with furniture that had come down from father, grandfather, and great-grandfather, with old family portraits, with mantels of beautiful design and carving, and a general assortment of old, family treasures. So do I recall another delightful hour with a charming young chatelaine whose house, with all its contents, including herself, I would gladly have carried away bodily had it been possible.

Too frequently the old equipment of the old house is divided among heirs, until the place is almost stripped and the rooms left bare and desolate, tenanted, perhaps, only by a maiden aunt or by some thriftless descendant with a dowdy wife. This stripping by division is common enough, but the occupants of the country houses are usually of good New England stock, and there is at least comfort and an air of home in the best meaning of the word. A few potted plants on the window-sill, and a cat of the kind described by Mark Twain, in *Pudd'n head Wilson*, as "a well-fed, well-petted, and properly revered cat," are simple but effective contributions to the making of a country home. The value of the cat, as a feature in home-making, is enhanced if there is a braided rug for it to lie upon in front of the fireplace. Somehow, the braided rug, made from cast-off garments, seems to fit admirably into the scheme of the interior of the old-time house, although it usually looks out of place elsewhere. It harmonizes with its environment and so fulfils a fundamental law of decoration.

It is to the taste and skill of carpenters, rather than to architects, that we are indebted for the grace and the charm of these old-time dwellings. Mr. Eberlein, an architect-author, in his book on *The Architecture of Colonial America*, says of them that "we shall not be far wrong in ascribing seventeenth-century buildings, almost without exception, to the capable and resourceful craftsman who not only preserved conscientiously the traditions he had learned as an apprentice or journeyman in the mother country, and faithfully perpetuated them by his practice as a master carpenter or joiner in a new land, but also showed himself possessed of ready wit and keen perceptive faculties by the alacrity with which he modified and adapted traditional methods and precedents to new conditions and requirements of climate and environment. Furthermore, these early workmen showed an all-round mastery of their craft. They respected their calling and took a proper pride in the excellence of their craftsmanship. Hence, the work of their hands, however plain and simple, still possesses a dignity and honest beauty that plainly proclaim how they put their hearts into what they were doing and, at the same time, commands our reverence and admiration."

Of the same class in the eighteenth century, to whom we owe much of the work of that period, the same writer says: "The master carpenter of the eighteenth century was infinitely more capable than the average artisan of like rank to-day. He was not only a skilled master mechanic, competent to translate rough drafts and sketches into carefully prepared working drawings, but he was also a person of some architectural education and taste and endowed with a nice perception of architectural merits and proprieties."

These were the men who, for the first two hundred years of life in New England, built the homes of the people. Little of their work remains in the cities, but much still stands in the villages and in country regions, monuments to an instructive past and charming features in a picturesque landscape.

PLATES

Providence, Rhode Island

Ives House, 1799

Providence, Rhode Island   *Gammell House, 1786*

Lexington, Massachusetts. The house in which Samuel Adams and John Hancock were asleep when aroused by Paul Revere

CPSIA information can be obtained at www.ICGtesting.com
Printed in the USA
BVOW06s1436060616

450920BV00014B/54/P